Kevin Garnett

By Jeffrey Zuehlke

AMAZING ATHLETES

LERNER**SPORTS** / Minneapolis

This book is available in two editions:
Library binding by LernerSports
Soft cover by First Avenue Editions
Imprints of Lerner Publishing Group
241 First Avenue North
Minneapolis, MN 55401 U.S.A.

Website address: www.lernerbooks.com

Library of Congress Cataloging-in-Publication Data

Zuehlke, Jeffrey, 1968–
    Kevin Garnett / by Jeffrey Zuehlke.
        p.   cm. — (Amazing athletes)
    Includes bibliographical references and index.
    ISBN: 0–8225–2429–5 (lib. bdg. : alk. paper)
    ISBN: 0–8225–2224–1 (pbk. : alk. paper)
    1. Garnett, Kevin, 1976– —Juvenile literature. 2. Basketball players—United States—Biography—Juvenile literature. I. Title. II. Series.
    GV884.G3Z84 2005
    796.323'092—dc22   2004001600

Manufactured in the United States of America
1 2 3 4 5 6 – JR – 10 09 08 07 06 05

TABLE OF CONTENTS

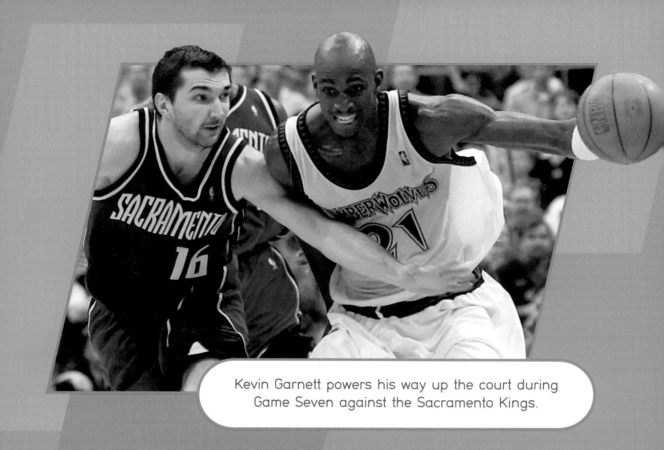

Kevin Garnett powers his way up the court during
Game Seven against the Sacramento Kings.

DOING IT ALL

Minnesota Timberwolves **forward** Kevin
Garnett caught the ball near the basket.
Players from the Sacramento Kings swarmed
around him. They wanted to keep Kevin from
scoring. With amazing quickness, he **dribbled**,

spun around, and shot. The ball sailed through the hoop. Two points!

The crowd exploded with cheers. Kevin's Timberwolves were playing in front of their home crowd in Minneapolis, Minnesota. The Wolves were facing the Sacramento Kings in Game Seven of the 2004 National Basketball Association (NBA) Western **Conference** Semifinals. The winner of the game would go on to the Western Conference **Finals.**

The winner of the conference finals would battle the Eastern Conference winner in the NBA Finals. Whichever team won the NBA Finals would be the best team in the NBA.

Kevin and the Minnesota Timberwolves play home games at the Target Center in Minneapolis.

Kevin leaps over Kings' center Brad Miller for a slam dunk.

Kevin led his team with great play after great play. Early in the fourth quarter, he charged past a defender. He dribbled straight to the hoop for a monster **slam dunk.** Later, he nailed a huge **three-point basket** to keep the Wolves in the lead.

Kevin didn't just score. As usual, he also played super defense, grabbing 21 **rebounds.** The Timberwolves won the game, 83–80. The crowd went wild! Kevin celebrated with his teammates. Kevin had an extra reason to be happy. It was May 19, 2004—his 28th birthday!

After the game, everyone was talking about Kevin's super performance. "He was scoring, he was rebounding, he was **blocking** shots," said Wolves forward Mark Madsen. "He was doing it all."

After the close win against the Kings, Kevin howls as the fans celebrate.

A Gift for the Game

Kevin Garnett was born on May 19, 1976, in Greenville, South Carolina. His mother, Shirley Garnett, worked in a factory. Kevin has two sisters, Sonya and Ashley.

Kevin's father, O'Lewis McCullough, didn't live with Kevin's family. Kevin didn't see his father much, but they shared one thing. Both of them loved basketball. O'Lewis had been a great player as a young man. Kevin soon showed he had a gift for the game too. Kevin played basketball as often as he could.

In 1988, when Kevin was twelve years old, the Garnetts moved to Mauldin, South

Carolina. Kevin's neighbor across the street, Jaime "Bug" Peters, also loved basketball. Kevin and Bug became best friends. They spent most of their free time on the basketball court.

By this time, Kevin was growing fast. He was already taller than most of the kids his age. Being tall helped Kevin to beat other kids in **pickup games.** He could shoot over other kids and block their shots. He could even jump high enough to make slam dunks.

As a kid, Kevin's favorite player was Magic Johnson of the Los Angeles Lakers.

In 1991, when Kevin entered Mauldin High School, he was six feet seven inches tall. He was a natural for the school's basketball team, the Mavericks. Kevin dreamed of playing for a big-time college team or even in the NBA.

Kevin wore number 21 when he played for Mauldin High School. He was a lot taller than most of the other players.

Kevin played with energy and emotion in high school.

ALL-AROUND PLAYER

Basketball is a team sport. To win, every player has to do his or her job. Kevin understood this. He always tried to give his teammates chances to play better. He wasn't a ball hog. Instead, he passed the ball to the teammate who had the best shot. Kevin's style made the Mavericks a winning team.

Kevin moved to
Chicago, Illinois, in 1994.
He led Farragut
Academy's Admirals to a
winning season.

In 1994, Kevin and his family moved to
Chicago, Illinois. For his senior year in high
school, Kevin went to Farragut Academy. He
soon became the basketball team's star player.
With Kevin leading the way, the Farragut
Admirals won 28 games and lost only 2. Kevin
averaged 28 points per game.

By this time, basketball experts were calling Kevin the best high school player in the country. All the big college basketball programs wanted him. But to get into these programs, Kevin had to pass a college test. But taking tests made him nervous, and he got bad scores.

Yet Kevin had another choice. Some basketball experts said Kevin was good enough to skip college and go straight to the NBA. Others said this would be bad for Kevin because he was too young. Kevin thought he could make it in the NBA. He decided to try to enter the NBA **draft.**

Before the draft, Kevin showed off his skills for NBA teams. Throughout June 1995, he played in several practice games called scrimmages.

NBA scouts and coaches loved Kevin's skills. The Minnesota Timberwolves wanted Kevin on their team. They chose him as the fifth pick in the 1995 draft.

Kevin was going to play against the world's best basketball players. Was he good enough to win against them?

Kevin was the first player in twenty years to go straight from high school to the NBA.

Kevin shows his serious focus during a game against the Los Angeles Lakers in 1995.

DA KID

Kevin began his rookie season in November 1995. The Timberwolves knew Kevin had a lot to learn. So they didn't put too much pressure on him. For the first half of the season, Kevin spent a lot of time on the bench. He watched and learned. He played just a few minutes every night.

Kevin learned fast. He practiced hard. And the Wolves' coaches and fans liked him. Kevin was always smiling and having fun. Because he was so young, people called him Da Kid. The nickname stuck.

Kevin likes all his nicknames. But most people call him by his initials, KG.

By the second half of the season, Da Kid was in the starting lineup. He blocked shots and grabbed rebounds. He threw down thunderous slam dunks.

Kevin's spectacular slam dunks entertain fans.

In his first season, Kevin shows
off his ballhandling in a game
against the Miami Heat.

Kevin made the NBA All-Star Team in only his second season. At twenty years old, he was the second youngest All-Star ever. That same season, the Wolves had drafted talented **point guard** Stephon Marbury. Stephon's speed and shooting skill gave the Wolves two star

Stephon Marbury brought a spark to the Wolves in the 1996–1997 season.

Kevin charms a Japanese fan at an off-season basketball camp.

players. Kevin and Stephon led the Timberwolves to their first-ever **playoff** appearance in 1997.

By this time, Kevin had become one of the NBA's most popular players. Fans all over the world were wearing his number 21 Timberwolves jersey. They loved how he played hard and always had a smile on his face. They cheered his powerful slam dunks.

Kevin talks with reporters after signing a huge new contract to stay with the Minnesota Timberwolves.

The Timberwolves wanted to keep Kevin on the team for a long time. During the summer of 1997, the team offered him a new **contract** that was worth $126 million! Kevin signed the deal. The big contract earned him a new nickname—the Big Ticket. Thousands of Timberwolves fans were buying tickets to see Kevin play.

Kevin faces off against forward Tracy Murray in 1997.

Kevin gave his best effort in the 1998 playoffs against the Seattle SuperSonics.

THE BIG TICKET

Kevin worked hard to earn his money. He was still a good team player. He made smart passes and played tough defense. He was named to the All-Star Team for the second year in a row. The Wolves made the 1998 playoffs again. They played hard but lost to the powerful Seattle SuperSonics in five games.

Kevin and the Timberwolves had some problems in the 1998–1999 season. Stephon said he didn't like playing in snowy Minnesota. So the Timberwolves **traded** him to the New Jersey Nets. Kevin was disappointed. Without Stephon, Kevin was the only superstar player on the team. The Wolves still had good players, but they weren't good enough to beat the best teams in the league.

The next four seasons, Kevin and the Wolves continued to play great basketball. They made the playoffs four years straight. But each year they faced better and stronger teams. The Wolves always came up second best.

In 2000, Kevin played for the U.S. basketball team at the Olympic Games in Sydney, Australia. Team USA won the gold medal. Kevin's high-energy play made him a fan favorite.

By 2003, Kevin was getting frustrated. He wanted to win an NBA Championship. But the Wolves didn't have enough good players. Before the 2003–2004 season, the Wolves traded some players to get better. They picked up two terrific guards, Latrell Sprewell and Sam Cassell. Meanwhile, Kevin decided to sign a new contract to stay with the Wolves for the next five years.

Kevin shows his frustration during the 2000–2001 season, when the Wolves again lost in the first round of the playoffs.

The addition of Sam Cassell *(left)* and Latrell Sprewell *(center)* gave Kevin and the Wolves a great chance to win in the 2003–2004 season.

With Kevin, Sam, and Latrell leading the way, the Wolves stormed through the regular season. They won 58 games and finished with the most wins of any NBA team in the Western Conference.

Kevin holds up the 2004 MVP trophy. The award goes to the year's best player in the NBA.

Kevin had a monster season. He led the league in total points and total rebounds. To top off the season, he was voted the NBA's Most Valuable Player (MVP).

Playing for a powerhouse team, Kevin had hopes of winning the NBA Finals. The Wolves rolled over the Denver Nuggets in the first series of the playoffs. Then they defeated the Sacramento Kings in an exciting seven-game series in the Western Conference Semifinals.

Kevin points to the Minnesota fans after the Wolves defeated the Kings in Game Seven. He scored 32 points, had 21 rebounds, and made 5 blocks.

But Kevin and the Wolves came up short against the Los Angeles Lakers in the Western Conference Finals, losing four games to two. He and his team would not get to play in the NBA Finals.

Kevin was disappointed but happy about the team's successful season. "We've got a good thing going," he said. "We've just got to add to it." With Kevin leading the way, the Wolves have many exciting seasons ahead.

Kevin poses with his wife, Brandi. They met in 1996 and married in 2004.

Selected Career Highlights

2003–2004
Voted NBA MVP
Led the NBA in total rebounds
Led the NBA in total points scored
Led the NBA in **double-doubles**, with 71
Became the first player to be named Player
   of the Month four times in one season

2002–2003
Voted MVP of the 2003 NBA All-Star Game
Named to All-NBA First Team
Named to All-NBA Defensive First Team

2001–2002
Selected to fifth NBA All-Star Game
Named to All-NBA Defensive First Team
Named to All-NBA Second Team

2000–2001
Selected to fourth NBA All-Star Game
Named to All-NBA Defensive First Team
Named to All-NBA Second Team

1999–2000
Selected to NBA All-Star Game
Named to All-NBA Defensive First Team
Won gold medal as member of the U.S. basketball team at
   2000 Olympic Games in Sydney, Australia

1998–1999
Named to All-NBA Third Team

1997–1998
Voted as starter to his second NBA All-Star Game

1996–1997
Selected for NBA All-Star Game

1995–1996
Named to NBA All-Rookie Second Team

1994–1995
Named National High School Player of the Year by *USA Today*
Named Mr. Basketball of Illinois, as the best player in the state
Played in the 1995 McDonald's All-American Game

Glossary

blocking: stopping another player's shot from going in the hoop

conference: one of the two groups of teams in the NBA. The groups are the Western Conference and the Eastern Conference. The winner of the Western Conference Finals meets the winner of the Eastern Conference Finals in the NBA Finals.

contract: a written deal signed by a player and his or her team. The player agrees to play for the team for a stated number of years. The team agrees to pay the player a stated amount of money.

double-double: making ten or more contributions in two categories in the same game. For example, a player who makes 10 points and 12 rebounds has a double-double.

draft: a yearly event in which all professional teams in a sport are given the chance to pick new players from a selected group

dribble: the continuous bouncing of the ball, using one hand

finals: the last set of games in the NBA playoffs. The winner of the NBA Finals is the best team in the NBA for the season.

forward: a player on a basketball team who usually plays close to the basket. Forwards need to rebound and shoot the ball well.

pickup game: a casual game, not run by a league or organization

playoffs: a series of contests played after the regular season has ended

point guard: a player on a basketball team who directs the other players and who handles the ball most of the time

rebound: grabbing the ball off the hoop or the backboard after a missed shot

rookie: a player who is playing his or her first season

slam dunk: putting the ball forcefully through the hoop, instead of shooting it in an arc through the air

three-point basket: a long-range shot that is worth three points. Shots closer to the basket are worth two points.

trade: to exchange a player on one team for a player on another team or for other benefits

Further Reading & Websites

Aschburner, Steve. *NBA All-Star Kevin Garnett*. New York: Scholastic, 2001.

Stewart, Mark. *Kevin Garnett: Shake Up the Game*. Brookfield, CT: Millbrook Press, 2002.

Torres, John A. *Kevin Garnett: "Da Kid."* Minneapolis: LernerSports, 2000.

4XL—For Excellence in Leadership
<http://4xl.monster.com/>
The website for Kevin's 4XL Foundation lists the organization's leadership and business programs for high school students, college students, and educators.

Minnesota Timberwolves Website
<http://www.nba.com/timberwolves/>
The official website of the Timberwolves includes team schedules, late-breaking news, profiles of past and present players, and much more.

Official Kevin Garnett Website
<http://www.upperdeck.com/athletes/kevingarnett/>
E-mail a question to Kevin at his official website. The site also lists his career highlights, photos, quotes, links to news stories, and information about his 4XL—For Excellence in Leadership Foundation.

Official NBA Website
<http://www.nba.com>
The official website of the National Basketball Association has all the latest NBA news, scores, schedules, and statistics, as well as biographies of players and coaches, and stories about the history of the NBA.

Sports Illustrated for Kids
<http://www.sikids.com>
The *Sports Illustrated for Kids* website covers all sports, including basketball.

Index

Photo Acknowledgments

AP/Wide World Photos, pp. 4, 6, 7, 15, 16, 18, 19, 20, 21, 22, 25, 26, 27; Classmates.com Yearbook Archives, p. 9; © Gwinn Davis/The Tribune-Times, pp. 10, 11; © Illinois High School Association, p. 12; © Marc Asnin/CORBIS SABA, p. 17; © Reuters/CORBIS, p. 24; © Rena Durham-KPA/ZUMA Press, p. 28;.© Icon SMI, p. 29.

Cover image: © Icon SMI